MW01115161

# One Pot Budget Cookbook
### Third edition

## By Don Orwell

http://SuperfoodsToday.com

## Your Free Gift

As a way of saying thanks for your purchase, I'm offering you my FREE eBook that is exclusive to my book and blog readers.

**Superfoods Cookbook - Book Two** has over 70 Superfoods recipes and complements Superfoods Cookbook Book One and it contains Superfoods Salads, Superfoods Smoothies and Superfoods Deserts with ultra-healthy non-refined ingredients. All ingredients are 100% Superfoods.

It also contains Superfoods Reference book which is organized by Superfoods (more than 60 of them, with the list of their benefits), Superfoods spices, all vitamins, minerals and antioxidants. Superfoods Reference Book lists Superfoods that can help with 12 diseases and 9 types of cancer.

http://www.SuperfoodsToday.com/FREE

# Table of Contents

## Introduction

Hello,

My name is Don Orwell and my blog SuperfoodsToday.com is dedicated to Superfoods Lifestyle.

One Pot Meals fit perfectly with a Superfoods Lifestyle. Superfoods cuisine means eating the most nutrition dense food for every meal and not eating processed food.

Luckily, there are so many cheap superfoods!! Superfoods Lifestyle means swapping bouillon cubes, gravy mix, garlic salt, pasta, potato, corn cans, beans cans and cream of mushroom canned soups for the whole foods Superfoods. Hey, tons of everyday Superfoods can be frozen and dumped in a pot or casserole for a quick dump dinner. I swapped expensive ingredients for less expensive ones and I hope that you will enjoy 100% Superfoods recipes that I prepared for you.

## Superfoods One Pot Meals

Allergy labels: SF – Soy Free, GF – Gluten Free, DF – Dairy Free, EF – Egg Free, V - Vegan, NF – Nut Free

## Overnight Cocoa Oatmeal Breakfast

Serves 4 - Allergies: SF, GF, NF

- 1 cup steel cut oatmeal

- 4 cups milk

- 1 tsp. of ground flax seeds

- 4 Tbsp. honey

- 1 tsp. of sunflower seeds

- A dash of cinnamon and/or nutmeg

- Half of the tsp. of cocoa

Oil slow cooker dish. Mix all ingredients in a mixing bowl, stir and put in the slow cooker. Cook on low for 8 hours. Stir before serving.

## Overnight Strawberries Oatmeal

*Serves 4*

*Ingredients - Allergies: SF, GF, DF, NF*

- 1 cup steel cut oatmeal
- 4 cups water
- 1 tsp. of ground flax seeds
- 4 Tbsp. honey
- 1 tsp. of sunflower seeds
- A dash of cinnamon and/or nutmeg

Oil slow cooker dish. Mix all ingredients in a mixing bowl, stir and put in the slow cooker. Cook on low for 8 hours. Stir before serving.

Topping suggestions: sliced strawberries, blueberries or few almonds.

# Walnuts and Blueberry Vanilla Overnight Oats

*Serves 1*

*Ingredients - Allergies: SF, GF, EF, V, NF*

- 1 cup steel cut oatmeal
- 4 cups milk
- 4 Tbsp. honey
- 1 tsp. of sunflower seeds
- A dash of cinnamon and/or nutmeg

Oil slow cooker dish. Mix all ingredients in a mixing bowl, stir and put in the slow cooker. Cook on low for 8 hours. Stir before serving.

Top with blueberries and walnuts.

## Apple Oatmeal

*Serves 4*

- 1 cup steel cut oatmeal
- 4 cups water
- 4 Tbsp. honey
- 4 apples
- A dash of cinnamon and/or nutmeg

Oil slow cooker dish. Mix all ingredients in a mixing bowl, stir and put in the slow cooker. Cook on low for 8 hours. Stir before serving.

Top with apple and cinnamon.

## Peanut Butter Banana Oats

*Serves 4*

- 1 cup steel cut oatmeal
- 4 cups water
- 4 Tbsp. honey
- 4 bananas
- A dash of cinnamon and/or nutmeg
- 1/2 tbs. peanut butter

Oil slow cooker dish. Mix all ingredients in a mixing bowl, stir and put in the slow cooker. Cook on low for 8 hours. Stir before serving.

Top with banana and almond butter.

# Broths

Some recipes require a cup or more of various broths, vegetable, beef or chicken broth. I usually cook the whole pot and freeze it in one cup or half a cup chunks.

## Vegetable broth

Servings: 6 cups

*Ingredients*

- 1 tbsp. oil
- 1 large onion, chopped
- 2 stalks celery, including some leaves
- 2 large carrots, chopped
- 1 bunch green onions, chopped
- 8 cloves garlic, minced
- 8 sprigs fresh parsley
- 6 sprigs fresh thyme
- 2 bay leaves
- 1 tsp. salt
- 2 quarts water

*Instructions - Allergies: SF, GF, DF, EF, V, NF*

Put all ingredients in slow cooker and cook on low for 4 hours. Other ingredients to consider: broccoli stalk, celery root. Let cool to warm room temperature and strain. Keep chilled and use or freeze broth within a few days.

## Chicken Broth

*Ingredients*

- 4 lbs. fresh chicken (wings, necks, backs, legs, bones)
- 2 peeled onions or 1 cup chopped leeks
- 2 celery stalks
- 1 carrot
- 8 black peppercorns
- 2 sprigs fresh thyme
- 2 sprigs fresh parsley
- 1 tsp. salt

*Instructions - Allergies: SF, GF, DF, EF, NF*

Put all ingredients in slow cooker and cook on low for 6 hours. Let cool to warm room temperature and strain. Keep chilled and use or freeze broth within a few days.

# Beef Broth

*Ingredients*

- 4-5 pounds beef bones and few veal bones
- 1 pound of stew meat (chuck or flank steak) cut into 2-inch chunks
- Olive oil
- 1-2 medium onions, peeled and quartered
- 1-2 large carrots, cut into 1-2 inch segments
- 1 celery rib, cut into 1 inch segments
- 2-3 cloves of garlic, unpeeled
- Handful of parsley, stems and leaves
- 1-2 bay leaves
- 10 peppercorns

*Instructions - Allergies: SF, GF, DF, EF, NF*

Heat oven to 375°F. Rub olive oil over the stew meat pieces, carrots, and onions. Place stew meat or beef scraps, stock bones, carrots and onions in a large roasting pan. Roast in oven for about 45 minutes, turning everything half-way through the cooking.

Place everything from the oven in the slow cooker and cook on low for 6 hours. After cooking, remove the bones and vegetables from the pot. Strain the broth. Let cool to room temperature and then put in the refrigerator.

The fat will solidify once the broth has chilled. Discard the fat (or reuse it) and pour the broth into a jar and freeze it.

## Tomato paste

Some recipes (chili) require tomato paste. I usually prepare 20 or so liters at once (when tomato is in season, which is usually September) and freeze it.

*Ingredients*

- 5 lbs. chopped plum tomatoes
- 1/4 cup extra-virgin olive oil plus 2 tbsp.
- salt, to taste

*Instructions - Allergies: SF, GF, DF, EF, V, NF*

Heat 1/4 cup of the oil in a skillet over medium heat. Add tomatoes. Season with salt. Bring to a boil. Cook, stirring, until very soft, about 8 minutes.

Pass the tomatoes through the finest plate of a food mill. Push as much of the pulp through the sieve as possible and leave the seeds behind.

Cook in slow cooker for 4 hours on low.
Store sealed in an airtight container in the refrigerator for up to one month, or freeze, for up to 6 months.

## Curry Paste

This should not be prepared in advance, but there are several curry recipes that are using curry paste and I decided to take the curry paste recipe out and have it separately. So, when you see that the recipe is using curry paste, please go to this part of the book and prepare it from scratch or defrost of you have it frozen. Don't use processed curry pastes or curry powder; make it every time from scratch. Keep the spices in original form (seeds, pods), ground them just before making the curry paste. You can dry heat in the skillet cloves, cardamom, cumin and coriander and then crush them coarsely with mortar and pestle.

*Ingredients*

- 2 onions, minced
- 2 cloves garlic, minced
- 2 teaspoons fresh ginger root, finely chopped
- 6 whole cloves

- 2 cardamom pods
- 2 (2 inch) pieces cinnamon sticks, crushed
- 1 tsp. ground cumin
- 1 tsp. ground coriander
- 1 tsp. salt
- 1 tsp. ground cayenne pepper
- 1 tsp. ground turmeric

*Instructions - Allergies: SF, GF, DF, EF, V, NF*

Heat oil in a frying pan over medium heat and fry onions until transparent. Stir in garlic, cumin, ginger, cloves, cinnamon, coriander, salt, cayenne, and turmeric. Cook for 1 minute over medium heat, stirring constantly. At this point other curry ingredients should be added or let cook and freeze.

## Healthy Superfoods Casserole Sauce

- 2 beaten eggs
- Salt, pepper
- 1 cup of low-fat Greek yogurt
- 1 Tbsp. olive oil
- 1/2 cup of low fat parmesan or shredded cheddar cheese

Optional:

- 1 tsp of flax seeds meal
- 1/2 tsp. oregano or thyme or any other herbs

## Precooked beans

Again, some recipes require that you cook some beans (butter beans, red kidney, garbanzo) in advance. Cooking beans takes around 3 hours and it can be done in advance or every few weeks and the rest get frozen. Soak beans for 24 hours before cooking them. After the first boil, throw the water, add new water and continue cooking. Some beans or lentils can be sprouted for few days before cooking and that helps if you have stomach problems.

# Soups

## Lentil Soup

*Serves 4-6*

*Ingredients - Allergies: SF, GF, DF, EF, NF*
- 2 tbsp. oil
- 1 cup finely chopped onion
- 1/2 cup chopped carrot
- 1/2 cup chopped celery
- 2 teaspoons salt
- 1 pound lentils
- 1 cup chopped tomatoes
- 2 quarts chicken or vegetable broth
- 1/2 tsp. ground coriander & toasted cumin

*Instructions*

Put all ingredients in the slow cooker and cook on low for 4 hours.

## Italian Beef Soup

*Serves 6*

*Ingredients - Allergies: SF, GF, DF, EF, NF*

- 1 pound minced beef
- 1 clove garlic, minced
- 2 cups beef broth
- few large tomatoes
- 1 cup sliced carrots
- 2 cups raw beans
- 2 small zucchini, cubed
- 2 cups spinach - rinsed and torn
- 1/4 tsp. black pepper
- 1/4 tsp. salt

Put all ingredients in slow cooker and cook on low for 8 hours.

## Black Bean Soup

*Serves 6-8*

*Ingredients - Allergies: SF, GF, DF, EF, NF*

- 1/4 cup oil
- 1/4 cup Onion, Diced
- 1/4 cup Carrots, Diced
- 1/4 cup Green Bell Pepper, Diced
- 1 cup beef broth
- 2 pounds raw Black Beans
- 1 tbsp. lemon juice
- 2 teaspoons Garlic
- 2 teaspoons Salt
- 1/2 tsp. Black Pepper, Ground
- 2 teaspoons Chili Powder
- 8 oz. pork
- 1 tbsp. flour
- 2 tbsp. Water

*Instructions*

Put all ingredients in slow cooker and cook on low for 8 hours.

## Squash soup

*Serves 4-6*

*Ingredients - Allergies: SF, GF, DF, EF, V, NF*

- 1 Squash, skin and seeds removed, chopped
- 1 carrot, chopped
- 1 onion (diced)
- 3/4 – 1 cup coconut milk
- 1/4 – 1/2 cup water
- oil
- Salt
- Pepper
- Cinnamon
- Turmeric

*Instructions*

Put all ingredients in the slow cooker and cook on low for 4 hours. Blend until smooth and creamy. Sprinkle it with toasted pumpkin seeds.

## Kale White Bean Pork Soup

*Serves 4-6*

*Ingredients - Allergies: SF, GF, DF, EF, NF*

- 2 tbsp. oil
- 3 tbsp. chili powder
- 1 tbsp. jalapeno hot sauce
- 2 pounds bone-in pork chops
- Salt
- 4 stalks celery, chopped
- 1 large white onion, chopped
- 3 cloves garlic, chopped
- 2 cups chicken broth
- 2 cups diced tomatoes
- 2 cups raw white beans
- 6 cups packed Kale

*Instructions*

Put all ingredients in the slow cooker and cook for 8 hours on low.

## Avgolemono – Greek lemon chicken soup
*Serves 4*

*Ingredients - Allergies: SF, GF, DF, EF, NF*

• 4 cups chicken broth

• 1/4 cup uncooked brown rice

• salt and pepper

• 3 eggs

• 3 tbsp. lemon juice

• Handful fresh dill (chopped)

• shredded roasted chicken (optional)

Whisk lemon juice and the eggs until smooth. Add about 1 cup of the hot broth into the egg/lemon mixture and whisk to combine.

Put all ingredients in the slow cooker and cook on low for 4 hours.

## Creamy Tomato Basil Soup

*Serves 6*

*Ingredients - Allergies: SF, GF, DF, EF, V, NF*

- 4 tomatoes - peeled, seeded and diced
- 4 cups tomato juice*
- 14 leaves fresh basil
- 1 cup heavy cream
- salt to taste
- ground black pepper to taste

*Instructions*

Put all ingredients in the slow cooker and cook on low for 4 hours.

## Minestrone

*Serves 8-10*

*Ingredients - Allergies: SF, GF, DF, EF, NF*

- 3 tbsp. oil
- 3 cloves garlic, chopped
- 2 onions, chopped
- 2 cups chopped celery
- 5 carrots, sliced
- 2 cups chicken broth
- 2 cups water
- 4 cups tomato sauce
- 1/2 oz. red wine (optional)
- 1 cup raw kidney beans
- 2 cups green beans
- 2 cups baby spinach, rinsed
- 3 zucchinis, quartered and sliced
- 1 tbsp. chopped oregano
- 2 tbsp. chopped basil
- salt and pepper to taste

*Instructions*

Put all ingredients in the slow cooker and cook on low for 6 hours.

# Superfoods Stews, Chilies and Curries

## Vegetarian Chili

*Serves 4-6*

*Ingredients - Allergies: SF, GF, DF, EF, V, NF*

1 tbsp. oil
1 cup chopped onions
3/4 cup chopped carrots
3 cloves garlic, minced
1 cup chopped green bell pepper
1 cup chopped red bell pepper
3/4 cup chopped celery
1 tbsp. chili powder
1-1/2 cups chopped mushrooms
3 cups chopped tomatoes
2 cups raw kidney beans
1 tbsp. ground cumin
1-1/2 teaspoons oregano
1-1/2 teaspoons crushed basil leaves

*Instructions*

Put all ingredients in the slow cooker and cook on low for 8 hours.

Lentil Stew

*Serves 6-8*

*Ingredients - Allergies: SF, GF, DF, EF, NF*

- 2 cup dry lentils
- 6 cups chicken broth
- a few tomatoes
- 1 medium potato chopped + 1/2 cup chopped carrot
- 1/2 cup chopped onion + 1/2 cup chopped celery (optional)
- a few sprigs of parsley and basil +  1 garlic clove (minced)
- 2 pound of cubed lean pork or beef + pepper to taste

**Instructions**: Dump everything in a slow cooker and cook on low for 3 hours.

Braised Green Peas with Beef

*Serves 4*

*Ingredients - Allergies: SF, GF, DF, EF, NF*

- 2 cups fresh or frozen green peas
- 2 onions, finely chopped
- 2 cloves of garlic, chopped and 1/2 inch of peeled and chopped fresh ginger (optional)
- 1/2 tsp. red pepper flakes, or to taste
- 1 tomato, roughly chopped
- 2 chopped carrots
- 2 tbsp. oil
- 1 cup chicken broth
- 1 pound cubed beef
- Salt and freshly ground black pepper (to taste)

Put all ingredients in the slow cooker and cook on low for 4 hours.

## White Chicken Chili
Serves: 5

*Ingredients - Allergies: SF, GF, DF, EF, NF*

- 4 large boneless, skinless chicken breasts
- 2 green bell peppers
- 1 large yellow onion
- 1 jalapeno
- 1/2 cup diced green chilies (optional)
- 1/2 cup of spring onions
- 1.5 tbsp. oil
- 3 cups cooked white beans
- 3.5 cups chicken or vegetable broth
- 1 tsp. ground cumin
- 1/4 tsp. cayenne pepper
- salt to taste

*Instructions*

Put all ingredients in the slow cooker and cook on low for 4 hours.

# Kale Pork

*Serves 4*

*Ingredients - Allergies: SF, GF, DF, EF, NF*

- 1 tbsp. oil
- 1 pound pork tenderloin, trimmed and cut into 1-inch pieces
- 3/4 tsp. salt
- 1 medium onion, finely chopped
- 4 cloves garlic, minced
- 2 teaspoons paprika
- 1/4 tsp. crushed red pepper (optional)
- 1 cup white wine
- 4 plum tomatoes, chopped
- 4 cups chicken broth
- 1 bunch kale, chopped
- 2 cups cooked white beans

*Instructions*

Put all ingredients in the slow cooker and cook on low for 4 hours.

Braised Green Beans with Pork

*Serves 2*

*Ingredients - Allergies: SF, GF, DF, EF, NF*

- 2 cups fresh or frozen green beans
- 1 onion, finely chopped
- 2 cloves of garlic, thinly sliced
- 1/2 inch of peeled/sliced fresh ginger
- 1/2 tsp. red pepper flakes, or to taste
- 1 tomato, roughly chopped
- 1 tbsp. oil
- 1/2 cup chicken broth
- Salt and ground black pepper
- 1/4 lemon, cut into wedges, to serve
- 1 pound lean pork

*Instructions*

Cut each bean in half. Put all ingredients in the slow cooker and cook on low for 4 hours.

## Barbecued Beef

*Serves 8*

*Ingredients - Allergies: SF, GF, DF, EF, NF*

- 1-1/2 cups tomato paste
- 1/4 cup lemon juice
- 2 tbsp. mustard
- 1/2 tsp. salt
- 1/4 tsp. ground black pepper
- 1/2 tsp. minced garlic
- 4 pounds boneless chuck roast

*Instructions*

Place chuck roast in a slow cooker. Pour all ingredients over and mix well. Cover, and cook on low for 7 to 9 hours.

## Superfoods Chili

*Serves 6*

*Ingredients - Allergies: SF, GF, DF, EF, NF*

- 2 tbsp. oil
- 2 onions, chopped
- 3 cloves garlic, minced
- 1 pound ground beef
- 3/4 pound beef sirloin, cubed
- 2cups diced tomatoes
- 1 cup strong brewed coffee
- 1cup tomato paste
- 2 cups beef broth
- 1 tbsp. cumin seeds
- 1 tbsp. unsweetened cocoa powder
- 1 tsp. dried oregano
- 1 tsp. ground cayenne pepper
- 1 tsp. ground coriander
- 1 tsp. salt
- 6 cups cooked kidney beans
- 4 fresh hot chili peppers, chopped

*Instructions*

Put all ingredients in the slow cooker and cook on low for 4 hours.

## Superfoods Goulash

*Serves 4-6*

*Ingredients - Allergies: SF, GF, DF, EF, NF*

- 3 cups cauliflower
- 1 pound ground beef
- 1 medium onion, chopped
- salt to taste
- ground black pepper to taste
- garlic to taste
- 2 cups cooked kidney beans
- 1 cup tomato paste

Put all ingredients in the slow cooker and cook on low for 4 hours.

## Frijoles Charros

*Serves 4-6*

*Ingredients - Allergies: SF, GF, DF, EF, NF*

- 1 pound precooked pinto beans
- 5 cloves garlic, chopped
- 1 tsp. salt
- 1/2 pound pork, diced
- 1 onion, chopped & 2 fresh tomatoes, diced
- few sliced sliced jalapeno peppers
- 1/3 cup chopped cilantro

*Instructions*

Put all ingredients in the slow cooker and cook on low for 4 hours.

Add cilantro before serving.

## Chicken Cacciatore

*Serves 8*

*Ingredients - Allergies: SF, GF, DF, EF, NF*

- 4 pounds of chicken thighs, with skin on
- 2 Tbsp. oil
- Salt
- 1 sliced onion
- 1/3 cup red wine
- 1 sliced red or green bell pepper
- 8 ounces sliced cremini mushrooms
- 2 sliced garlic cloves
- 3 cups peeled and chopped tomatoes
- 1/2 tsp. ground black pepper
- 1 tsp. dry oregano
- 1 tsp. dry thyme
- 1 sprig fresh rosemary
- 1 tbsp. fresh parsley

*Instructions*

Put all ingredients in the slow cooker and cook on low for 4 hours.

## Cabbage Stewed with Meat

*Serves 8*

*Ingredients - Allergies: SF, GF, DF, EF, NF*

- 1-1/2 pounds ground beef
- 1 cup beef stock
- 1 chopped onion
- 1 bay leaf
- 1/4 tsp. pepper
- 2 sliced celery ribs
- 4 cups shredded cabbage
- 1 carrot, sliced
- 1 cup tomato paste
- 1/4 tsp. salt

*Instructions*

Put all ingredients in the slow cooker and cook on low for 4 hours.

## Beef Stew with Peas and Carrots

*Serves 8*

*Ingredients - Allergies: SF, GF, DF, EF, NF*

- 1-1/2 cups chopped carrots
- 1 cup chopped onions
- 2 tbsp. oil
- 1-1/2 cups green peas
- 4 cups beef stock
- 1/2 tsp. salt
- 1/4 tsp. ground black pepper
- 1/2 tsp. minced garlic
- 4 pounds boneless chuck roast

*Instructions*

Put all ingredients in the slow cooker and cook on low for 6 hours.

## Green Chicken Stew

*Serves 6-8*

*Ingredients - Allergies: SF, GF, DF, EF, NF*

- 1-1/2 cups broccoli florets
- 1 cup chopped celery stalks
- 1 cup sliced leeks
- 2 tbsp. oil
- 1-1/2 cups green peas
- 2 cups chicken stock
- 1/2 tsp. salt
- 1/4 tsp. ground black pepper
- 1/2 tsp. minced garlic
- 4 pounds boneless skinless chicken pieces

*Instructions*

Put all ingredients in the slow cooker and cook on low for 4 hours.

## Irish Stew

*Serves 8*

*Ingredients - Allergies: SF, GF, DF, EF, NF*

- 2 chopped onions
- 2 Tbsp. oil
- 1 sprig dried thyme
- 2 1/2 pounds chopped meat from lamb neck
- 6 chopped carrots
- 2 tbsp. brown rice
- 5 cups chicken stock
- Salt
- Ground black pepper
- 1 Tbsp. each parsley and bay leaf
- 2 chopped sweet potatoes
- 1 bunch chopped parsley
- 1 bunch chives

*Instructions*

Put all ingredients in the slow cooker and cook on low for 6 hours.

## Hungarian Pea Stew

*Serves 8*

*Ingredients - Allergies: SF, GF, DF, EF, NF*

- 6 cups green peas
- 1 pound cubed pork
- 2 tbsp oil
- 3 1/2 tbsp flour
- 2 tbsp chopped parsley
- 1 cup water
- 1/2 tsp salt
- 1 cup coconut milk
- 1 tsp coconut sugar

*Instructions*

Put all ingredients in the slow cooker and cook on low for 6 hours.

## Greek Beef Stew (Stifado)

*Serves 8*

*Ingredients - Allergies: SF, GF, DF, EF, NF*

- 4 large pieces of veal or beef
- 20 whole shallots, peeled
- 3 bay leaves
- 8 garlic cloves
- 3 sprigs rosemary
- 6 whole pimento
- 5 whole cloves
- 1/2 tsp ground nutmeg
- 1/2 cup olive oil or avocado oil
- 1/3 cup apple cider vinegar
- 1 tbsp. salt
- 2 cups tomato paste
- 1/4 tsp black pepper

*Instructions*

Put all ingredients in the slow cooker and cook on low for 8 hours.

## Beef, Parsnip, Celery Stew

*Serves 8*

*Ingredients - Allergies: SF, GF, DF, EF, NF*

- 2 1/2 pounds cubed beef meat
- 2 chopped onions
- 6 chopped carrots
- 2 Tbsp. oil
- 1 sprig dried thyme
- 2 chopped parsnips
- 2 tbsp. brown rice
- 4 cups beef stock
- Salt
- Ground black pepper
- 1 bouquet garni (thyme, parsley and bay leaf)
- 1 bunch chopped parsley
- 1 bunch chives

*Instructions*

Put all ingredients in the slow cooker and cook on low for 8 hours.

## Chicken Mushrooms & Olives Stew

*Serves 6*

*Ingredients - Allergies: SF, GF, DF, EF, NF*

- 4 pounds chicken with skin on
- 1-1/2 cups chopped carrots
- 1 cup chopped onions
- 2 tbsp. oil
- 1 cup sliced mushrooms
- 1/2 cup chopped celery
- 1 cup black olives
- 1/2 tsp. salt
- 1/4 tsp. ground black pepper
- 1/2 tsp. minced garlic
- ½ cup fresh parsley

*Instructions*

Put all ingredients in the crockpot, cover and cook on low 6 hours.

### Chicken Pasanda Curry

Serves: 6

*Ingredients - Allergies: SF, GF, DF, EF, NF*

- 2 cups cubed chicken meat
- Curry Paste, but go low on the heat
- 2 cups tomato paste
- 1/2 cup heavy cream
- Cilantro for garnishing

*Instructions*

Make Curry Paste. Add the tomato paste, chicken and the cream. Stir to combine, add to crockpot and cook on low for 3 hours.

## Beef Meatballs with White Beans
*Serves 8*

*Ingredients - Allergies: SF, GF, DF, EF, NF*

- 2 pounds baked meatballs (see recipe in bonus chapter)
- 2 Tbsp. oil
- 1 sprig dried thyme
- 1 sprig dried thyme
- 2 cups uncooked white navy beans
- 4 cups beef stock
- Salt
- Ground black pepper
- 1 cup chopped onions
- 1 bunch chopped parsley
- 1 cup chopped carrots

*Instructions*

Add all ingredients but meatballs and cook on high for 4 hours. Add meatballs and cook on low for 2 hours more. Garnish with parsley.

## Stuffed Peppers with beans

*Serves 2*

*Ingredients - Allergies: SF, GF, NF*

2 large red or green bell peppers
2 cups stewed tomatoes
1/3 cup brown rice
2 tbsp. hot water
2 green onions
8 ounces cooked black beans
1/4 tsp. crushed red pepper flakes

*Instructions*

Discard seeds and membrane from peppers. Place cut-side down and cover. Bake at 375F for 15 minutes.
Mix 1 cup tomatoes, rice, thinly sliced green onions, beans and pepper flakes. Drain peppers. Turn cut-side up. Spoon tomato & beans mixture evenly into peppers, arrange peppers tight in the slow cooker. Pour slowly second cup of tomatoes between peppers, cover and cook on low for 4 hours.

## Slow cooked Squash, Cauliflower and Peppers Coconut Curry

Serves: 6

*Ingredients - Allergies: SF, GF, NF*

- Curry Paste – see recipe
- 3 cups peeled, chopped squash
- 1 cup heavy cream
- 3 tbsp. oil
- 1 tbsp. honey
- 2 pounds tomatoes
- 1 cup chopped Cauliflower
- 1 cup chopped Green Peppers
- Cilantro for topping

*Instructions*

Put all ingredients in the slow cooker and cook on low for 4 Hrs.

## Chickpea Curry

*Serves 4*

*Ingredients - Allergies: SF, GF, NF*

• Curry Paste

• 4 cups cooked chickpeas
• 1 cup chopped cilantro

*Instructions*

Put all ingredients in the slow cooker and cook on low for 4 Hrs.

# Ratatouille

*Serves 4-6*

*Ingredients - Allergies: SF, GF, NF*

- 2 large eggplants, sliced
- 2 medium onions, sliced
- 2 red or green peppers, sliced
- 4 large tomatoes, sliced
- 2 cloves garlic, crushed
- 4 tbsp. oil
- 1 tbsp. fresh basil
- Salt and freshly milled black pepper

*Instructions*

Put all ingredients in the slow cooker and cook on low for 4 Hrs.

## Pork, Celery and Basil Stew

*Serves 8*

*Ingredients - Allergies: SF, GF, DF, EF, NF*

- 1 cup chopped onions
- 2 Tbsp. coconut oil
- 2 1/2 pounds chopped pork meat
- 4 chopped carrots
- 2 cups beef stock
- 1 cup red wine (optional)
- Salt
- Ground black pepper
- 1 bunch chopped parsley
- 1 cup chopped celery
- 1/2 cup fresh basil

*Instructions*

Add all ingredients to slow cooker and cook on low for 8 hours.

## Pork Stew with Plums

*Serves 8*

*Ingredients - Allergies: SF, GF, DF, EF, NF*

- 1 cup chopped onions
- 2 Tbsp. oil
- 2 1/2 pounds chopped pork meat
- 2 chopped carrots
- 1 cup chicken stock
- 1 cup red wine (optional)
- Salt
- Ground black pepper
- 2 cups halved ripe plums, stoned
- 2 garlic cloves

*Instructions*

Add all ingredients to slow cooker and cook on low for 8 hours.

## Slow cooked Cabbage Rolls
*Serves 8*

*Ingredients - Allergies: SF, GF, DF, EF, NF*

1 cup  ground pork
1 cup chopped onion
1 liter tomato sauce
3 1/2 pounds cabbage or sauerkraut leaves
1 cup uncooked brown rice
1/2 cup millet
1/4 cup ground flax meal
1 tsp. salt
2 cups broth
*Instructions*

In a large mixing bowl combine onions, rice, flax, millet, ground pork and salt. Roll mixture into cabbage leaves and arrange them in a slow cooker dish. Pour broth and tomato sauce over rolls and cook on low for 4 hours.

## Slow cooked Chia, Flax & Broccoli
*Serves 4*

*Ingredients - Allergies: SF, GF, NF*

- 2 cups broccoli florets
- 1 cup chopped onions
- 2 tbsp. oil
- 1 cup Healthy Superfoods Casserole Sauce
- 1/2 cup flax seeds meal
- 1/2 cup chia seeds

*Instructions*

Put broccoli and onions in the slow cooker dish, mix sauce cream, flax and chia seeds, pour sauce on top, cover and cook on low for 3 hours.

## Slow cooked Sweet Potatoes & Tomato Casserole

*Serves 4*

*Ingredients - Allergies: SF, GF, NF*

- 1-1/2 cups chopped sweet potatoes
- 1 cup chopped onions
- 2 tbsp. oil
- 1-1/2 cups sliced tomatoes
- 1 cup Healthy Superfoods Casserole Sauce
- 1 Tbsp. chopped parsley

*Instructions*

Put all recipe ingredients (except sauce) in the slow cooker dish, pour sauce on top, arrange sliced tomatoes on top, cover and cook on low for 4 hours. Garnish with parsley.

## Slow cooked Eggplant, Zucchini and Tomato

*Serves 4*

*Ingredients - Allergies: SF, GF, DF, EF, NF*

- 1-1/2 cups sliced zucchini
- 1-1/2 cups sliced tomatoes
- 2 tbsp. oil
- 1-1/2 cups sliced eggplant
- 1/2 tsp. salt
- 1/4 tsp. ground black pepper
- 1/2 tsp. minced garlic

*Instructions*

Arrange all ingredients in the slow cooker dish, cover and cook on low for 4 hours.

## Slow cooked Zucchini

*Serves 4*

*Ingredients - Allergies: SF, GF, DF, EF, NF*

- 1-1/2 cups sliced zucchini
- 1 cup chopped onions
- 2 tbsp. oil
- 2 tbsp. chopped green onions
- 1 cup Healthy Superfoods Casserole Sauce

*Instructions*

Put ingredients in the casserole dish, pour sauce on top, cover and bake for 1 1/2 hours on 400F. Sprinkle with green onions before serving.

# Slow cooked Red Peppers, Zucchini and Eggplant

*Serves 4*

*Ingredients - Allergies: SF, GF, DF, EF, NF*

- 2 chopped carrots
- 1 - 1/2 cup chopped onions
- 1 - 1/2 cup sliced red peppers
- 4 tbsp. oil
- 1 cup sliced zucchini
- 1/2 tsp. salt
- 1/4 tsp. ground black pepper
- 1/2 tsp. minced garlic
- 1/2 tsp. oregano
- 2 pounds sliced eggplant
- 1 cup Tomato Paste

*Instructions*

Put all ingredients in the slow cooker and cook on low for 4 Hrs.

## Brown Rice Mushrooms Vegetarian Stew

*Serves 6-8*

*Ingredients - Allergies: SF, GF, DF, EF, NF*

- 2 chopped onions
- 2 Tbsp. oil
- 1 sprig dried thyme
- 6 chopped carrots
- 1 cup brown rice
- 2 cups mushrooms, sliced
- 4 cups chicken stock
- Salt
- Ground black pepper
- 1 bunch chopped parsley

*Instructions*

Put all ingredients in the slow cooker and cook on low for 4 Hrs.

## Vegetarian Garbanzo Chili
*Serves 8*

*Ingredients - Allergies: SF, GF, DF, EF, NF*

- 2 chopped onions
- 2 Tbsp. oil
- 3 large tomatoes, chopped
- 1 cup dry beans (kidney, black, pinto)
- 1 cup garbanzo beans
- 4 chopped carrots
- a few chopped jalapeno peppers (watch for the heat)
- 4 cups beef stock
- Salt
- Ground black pepper
- 1 bunch chopped spring onions

*Instructions*

Put all ingredients in the slow cooker and cook on low for 4 Hrs.

## Meat Stew with Red Beans

*Serves 8*

*Ingredients - Allergies: SF, GF, DF, EF, NF*

- 3 tbsp. oil
- 1/2 cup chopped onion
- 1 lb lean cubed stewing beef
- 2 tsp. ground cumin
- 2 tsp. ground turmeric (optional)
- 1/2 tsp. ground cinnamon (optional)
- 2 1/2 cups water
- 5 tbsp. chopped fresh parsley
- 3 tbsp. snipped chives
- 2 cups cooked kidney beans
- 1 lemon, juice of
- 1 tbsp. flour
- salt and black pepper

*Instructions*

Put all ingredients in the slow cooker and cook on low for 4 Hrs.

## Lamb and Sweet Potato Stew
*Serves 8*

*Ingredients - Allergies: SF, GF, DF, EF, NF*

- 1-1/2 cups tomato paste
- 1/4 cup lemon juice
- 2 tbsp. mustard
- 1/2 tsp. salt
- 1/4 tsp. ground black pepper
- 1/4 cup chunky almond butter
- 2 cubed sweet potatoes
- 1/2 tsp. minced garlic
- 4 pounds boneless chuck roast

*Instructions*

In a large bowl, combine tomato paste, lemon juice, almond butter and mustard. Stir in salt, pepper, garlic and cubed sweet potato.

Place chuck roast in a slow cooker. Pour tomato mixture over chuck roast. Cover, and cook on low for 7 to 9 hours.

## Slow Cooker Pepper Steak

*Serves 4-6*

*Ingredients - Allergies: SF, GF, DF, EF, NF*

- 2 pounds beef sirloin, cut into 2 inch strips
- 1 tbsp. minced garlic
- 3 tbsp. oil
- 1 cup Beef Broth

- 1 tbsp. tapioca flour
- 1/2 cup chopped onion
- 2 cups carrots
- 1 cup chopped tomatoes
- 1 tsp. salt

*Instructions*

Sprinkle beef with minced garlic. Heat the oil in a skillet and brown the seasoned beef sirloin strips. Transfer to a slow cooker. Add carrots, onion, chopped tomatoes and salt. Mix in tapioca flour in broth until dissolved. Pour broth into the slow cooker with meat. Cover and cook on high for 3 to 4 hours, or on low for 6 to 8 hours.

## Pork Tenderloin with peppers and onions
*Serves 3-4*

*Ingredients - Allergies: SF, GF, DF, EF, NF*

- 1 tbsp. oil
- 1 pound pork loin
- 1 tbsp. caraway seeds
- 1/2 tsp sea salt
- 1/4 tsp ground black pepper
- 1 red onion, thinly sliced
- 2 red bell peppers, sliced
- 4 cloves of garlic, minced
- 1/4-1/3 cup chicken broth

*Instructions*

Wash and chop vegetables. Slice pork loin, and season with black pepper, caraway seeds and sea salt. Heat a pan over medium heat. Add oil when hot. Add pork loin and brown slightly. Add onions and mushrooms, and continue to sauté until onions are translucent. Add peppers, garlic and chicken broth. Simmer until vegetables are tender and pork is fully cooked.

## Beef Bourguinon
*Serves 8-10*

*Ingredients - Allergies: SF, GF, DF, EF*

- 4 pounds cubed lean beef
- 1 cup red wine
- 1/3 cup oil
- 1 tsp. thyme
- 1 tsp. black pepper
- 2 cloves garlic, crushed
- 1 onion, diced
- 1 pound mushrooms, sliced
- 1/3 cup flour

*Instructions*

Marinate beef in wine, oil, thyme and pepper for few hours at room temperature or 6-8 hours in the fridge. Add beef with marinade and all other ingredients to a crock pot. Cook on low for 7-9 hrs.

# Italian Chicken

*Serves 6-8*

*Ingredients - Allergies: SF, GF, DF, EF*

- 1 skinless chicken, cut into pieces
- 1/4 cup flour
- 1 1/2 tsp. salt
- 1/8 tsp. pepper
- 1/2 cup chicken broth
- 1 cup sliced mushrooms
- 1/2 tsp. paprika
- 1 zucchini, sliced into medium pieces
- ground black pepper
- parsley to garnish

*Instructions*

Season chicken with 1 tsp. salt. Combine flour, pepper, remaining salt, and paprika. Coat chicken pieces with this mixture. Place zucchini first in a crockpot. Pour broth over zucchini. Arrange chicken on top. Cover and cook on low for 6 to 8 hours or until tender. Turn control to high, add mushrooms, cover, and cook on high for additional 10-15 minutes. Garnish with parsley and ground black pepper.

## Ropa Vieja

*Ingredients - Allergies: SF, GF, DF, EF, NF*

6 servings

- 1 tbsp. oil
- 2 pounds beef flank steak
- 1 cup beef broth
- 1 cup tomato sauce
- 1 small onion, sliced
- 1 green bell pepper sliced into strips
- 2 cloves garlic, chopped
- 1/2 cup tomato paste
- 1 tsp. ground cumin
- 1 tsp. chopped cilantro
- 1 tbsp. olive oil & 1 tbsp. lemon juice

*Instructions*

Add all ingredients to a crock pot. Cover, and cook on high for 4 hours, or on Low for up to 8 hours.

## Lemon Roast Chicken

*Serves 6-8*

*Ingredients - Allergies: SF, GF, DF, EF, NF*

- 1 whole skinless chicken
- 1 dash Salt
- 1 dash Pepper
- 1 tsp. Oregano
- 2 cloves minced garlic
- 2 tbsp. oil
- 1/4 cup Water
- 3 tbsp. Lemon juice
- Rosemary

*Instructions*

Add ingredients to a crock pot and cover. Cook on low 7 hours. Add lemon juice when cooking is done.

## Fall Lamb and Vegetable Stew
*Serves 6-8*

*Ingredients - Allergies: SF, GF, DF, EF, NF*

- 2 pounds Lamb stew meat
- 2 chopped Tomatoes
- 1 Summer squash
- 1 Zucchini
- 1 cup Mushrooms, sliced
- 1/2 cup Bell peppers, chopped
- 1 cup Onions, chopped
- 2 teaspoons Salt
- 1 each Garlic cloves, crushed
- 1/2 tsp. Thyme leaves
- 1 each Bay leaves
- 2 cups chicken broth

*Instructions*

Cut squash and zucchini. Place vegetables and lamb in crockpot. Mix salt, garlic, thyme, and bay leaf into broth and pour over lamb and vegetables. Cover and cook on low for 7 hours. Serve over brown rice.

## Slow cooker pork loin

*Serves 4-6*

*Ingredients - Allergies: SF, GF, DF, EF, NF*

- 1-1/2 lb pork loin
- 1 cup tomato sauce
- 2 zucchinis, sliced
- 1 head cauliflower, separated into medium florets
- 1-2 Tbs dried basil
- 1/4 tsp ground black pepper
- 1/2 tsp sea salt (optional)

*Instructions*

Add all of the ingredients to a crock pot.

Cook on high for 3-4 hours or low 7-8 hours.

## Pork, Zucchini, Pork, Tomato & Corn Stew

*Serves 8*

*Ingredients - Allergies: SF, GF, DF, EF, NF*

- 1-1/2 cups cooked corn
- 1 cup chopped onions
- 1-1/2 cups sliced zucchini
- 1-1/2 cups chopped tomato
- 2 tbsp. oil
- 2 tbsp. chopped garlic
- 2 tsp. salt and 1 tsp. ground pepper
- 4 pounds cubed pork

*Instructions*

Put ingredients in the slow cooker. Cover, and cook on low for 7 to 9 hours.

## Red Peppers Pork Curry

*Serves 8*

*Ingredients - Allergies: SF, GF, DF, EF, NF*

- 3 cups sliced red peppers
- 2 cups chopped onions
- 2 tbsp. oil
- 1 cup curry paste*
- 4 pounds chopped pork meat

*Instructions*

Put ingredients in the slow cooker. Cover, and cook on low for 7 to 9 hours.

## Beef Ratatouille

*Serves 8*

*Ingredients - Allergies: SF, GF, DF, EF, NF*

- 1-1/2 cups sliced zucchini
- 1 cup chopped onions
- 1-1/2 cups sliced eggplant
- 1-1/2 cups sliced red peppers (or tomato)
- 2 tbsp. oil
- 2 tbsp. chopped garlic
- 2 tsp. salt and 1 tsp. ground pepper
- 4 pounds cubed beef

*Instructions*

Put ingredients in the slow cooker. Cover, and cook on low for 7 to 9 hours.

## Chicken, Green Peas and Red Peppers Stew

*Serves 8*

*Ingredients - Allergies: SF, GF, DF, EF, NF*

- 1-1/2 cups green peas
- 1 cup chopped onions
- 1-1/2 cups sliced red peppers
- 2 tbsp. oil
- 2 cups chicken broth
- 2 tsp. salt and 1 tsp. ground pepper
- 4 pounds cubed chicken

*Instructions*

Put ingredients in the slow cooker. Cover, and cook on low for 7 to 9 hours.

## Crock Pot Turkey Roast Mediterranean style
*Serves 8*

*Ingredients - Allergies: SF, GF, DF, EF, NF*

- 1/2 cup Kalamata olives
- 1/2 cup chopped sun dried tomatoes
- 1 cup chicken broth
- 3 garlic cloves, minced
- 2 cups chopped onions
- 2 tbsp. oil
- 4 pounds turkey breast
- Rub thyme, salt and ground black pepper.

*Instructions*

Put ingredients in the slow cooker. Cover, and cook on low for 7 to 9 hours.

## Slow Cooker Pot Roast

*Serves 8*

*Ingredients - Allergies: SF, GF, DF, EF, NF*

- 1 cup sliced celery
- 1 cup chopped carrot
- 3 cups beef broth
- 1 cup red wine (optional) & 3 garlic cloves (optional)
- 1 cup chopped onions
- 2 tbsp. oil
- 4 pounds beef chuck roast
- Rub thyme, salt and ground black pepper. Add 1 bay leaf.

*Instructions*

Put ingredients in the slow cooker. Cover, and cook on low for 7 to 9 hours.

## Crock Pot Whole Chicken
*Serves 8*

*Ingredients - Allergies: SF, GF, DF, EF, NF*

- 1 cup sliced celery
- 1 cup chopped carrot
- 1 cup chopped parsnip (optional)
- 2 cups chopped onions
- 2 tbsp. oil
- 1 whole chicken with skin on
- Rub paprika, salt and ground black pepper on the chicken skin and inside. Optionally add lemon quarters inside.

*Instructions*

Put veggies in the slow cooker and place chicken on top. Cover, and cook on low for 7 to 9 hours.

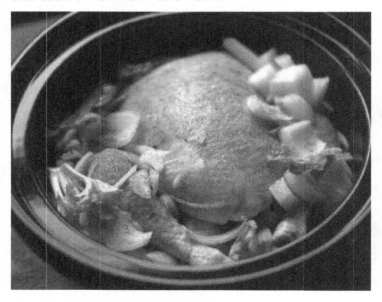

## Chicken in Sun Dried Tomato Sauce
*Serves 8*

*Ingredients - Allergies: SF, GF, DF, EF, NF*

- 12 sun dried tomatoes, chopped
- 1 cup heavy milk
- 1 cup chicken broth
- 1/2 cup white wine (optional)
- a pinch of dried thyme and oregano
- 2 tbsp. oil
- Salt and ground black pepper to taste
- 4 pounds dark chicken meat

*Instructions*

Put ingredients in the slow cooker. Cover, and cook on low for 7 to 9 hours.

## Corn, Mushrooms Chicken Stew

*Serves 8*

*Ingredients - Allergies: SF, GF, DF, EF, NF*

- 2 cups sliced mushrooms
- 2 cups chopped onions
- 2 cups corn
- 2 tbsp. oil
- 3 cups tomato paste*
- Salt and ground black pepper to taste
- 4 pounds chicken meat

*Instructions*

Put ingredients in the slow cooker. Cover, and cook on low for 7 to 9 hours.

## Chicken and Baby Carrots Stew

*Serves 8*

*Ingredients - Allergies: SF, GF, DF, EF, NF*

- 3 cups baby carrots
- 2 cups chopped onions
- 2 tbsp. oil
- Salt, ground black pepper to taste
- 4 pounds dark chicken meat

*Instructions*

Put ingredients in the slow cooker. Cover, and cook on low for 7 to 9 hours.

## Black Bean, Chicken & Brown Rice Stew

*Serves 8*

*Ingredients - Allergies: SF, GF, DF, EF, NF*

- 1 cup brown rice
- 1 cup chopped onions
- 2 tbsp. oil
- 1 cup uncooked black beans
- Salt, ground black pepper and ground cumin to taste
- 4 cups chicken stock
- 4 pounds chicken breast meat cut into stripes

*Instructions*

Put ingredients in the slow cooker. Cover, and cook on low for 7 to 9 hours.

## Pork White Bean Chili

*Serves 8*

*Ingredients - Allergies: SF, GF, DF, EF, NF*

- 2 cups sliced red peppers
- 2 cups chopped onions
- 2 tbsp. oil
- 1 cup uncooked white beans
- ¼ cup sliced jalapeno peppers (adjust heat to taste)
- 1 cup sweet corn
- Salt, ground black pepper and ground cumin to taste
- 2-3 cups beef stock
- 4 pounds minced pork meat

*Instructions*

Put ingredients in the slow cooker. Cover, and cook on low for 7 to 9 hours.

## Pork Meat Stew

*Serves 8*

*Ingredients - Allergies: SF, GF, DF, EF, NF*

- 3 large tomatoes, sliced
- 1 cup chopped onions
- 2 tbsp. oil
- 2 large red peppers, sliced
- 1 bunch chopped parsley
- Salt, ground black pepper and ground cumin to taste
- 1 cup beef stock
- 4 pounds cubed pork meat

*Instructions*

Put ingredients in the slow cooker. Cover, and cook on low for 7 to 9 hours.

## Lamb & Zucchini Stew

*Serves 8*

*Ingredients - Allergies: SF, GF, DF, EF, NF*

- 2 medium zucchinis, sliced
- 1 cup chopped onions
- 2 tbsp. oil
- 2 sliced tomatoes & 2 yellow peppers, sliced
- 2 Tbsp. chopped rosemary
- Salt, ground black pepper and ground cumin to taste
- 1 cup beef stock
- 4 pounds cubed lamb meat

*Instructions*

Put ingredients in the slow cooker. Cover, and cook on low for 7 to 9 hours.

## Chicken, Mushrooms & Carots Stew
*Serves 8*

*Ingredients - Allergies: SF, GF, DF, EF, NF*

- 2 cups halved mushrooms
- 1 cup chopped onions
- 2 tbsp. oil
- 2 cups chopped carrots
- Salt, ground black pepper to taste
- 1 cup chicken stock
- 4 pounds cubed chicken meat

*Instructions*

Put ingredients in the slow cooker. Cover, and cook on low for 7 to 9 hours.

## Cabbage & Mushrooms Beef Stew

*Serves 8*

*Ingredients - Allergies: SF, GF, DF, EF, NF*

- 2 cups sliced mushrooms
- 1 cup chopped onions & 1 cup chopped carrot
- 2 tbsp. oil
- 2 cups sauerkraut
- Salt, ground black pepper and ground cumin to taste
- 2 cups beef stock
- 2 pounds ground beef

*Instructions*

Put ingredients in the slow cooker and mix. Cover, and cook on low for 7 to 9 hours.

## Brown Mushrooms & Chicken Stew

*Serves 8*

*Ingredients - Allergies: SF, GF, DF, EF, NF*

- 2 cups whole brown mushrooms
- 1 cup chopped leeks
- 2 tbsp. oil
- Salt, ground black pepper to taste
- 3 cups chicken stock
- 4 pounds cubed chicken meat

*Instructions*

Put ingredients in the slow cooker. Cover, and cook on low for 7 to 9 hours.

## Creamy Mushroom Chicken Stew

*Serves 8*

*Ingredients - Allergies: SF, GF, DF, EF, NF*

- 1 cup full fat coconut milk
- 1 cup chopped onions & 2 garlic cloves, minced
- 4 tbsp. oil
- 1 cup chopped carrot
- Salt, ground black pepper and fresh thyme to taste
- 3 cups mixed Portobello and white button mushrooms
- 1 cup beef stock
- 4 pounds chopped chicken meat

*Instructions*

Put ingredients in the slow cooker. Cover, and cook on low for 7 to 9 hours.

# Ground Chicken & Brown Rice Stuffed Peppers

*Serves 8*

*Ingredients - Allergies: SF, GF, DF, EF, NF*

- 2 cups brown rice
- 2 cup chopped onions
- 2 tbsp. oil
- Salt, ground black pepper and ground cumin to taste
- 4 cups chicken stock
- 3 pounds ground chicken
- 16 large green, yellow and red peppers

*Instructions*

Mix chopped onions, ground meat and brown rice. Cut off the peppers stems and fill peppers with the mixture. Arrange peppers in the slow cooker and pour stock between peppers. Cover, and cook on low for 7 to 9 hours.

## Slow Cooked Paella

*Serves 6-8*

*Ingredients - Allergies: SF, GF, DF, EF, NF*

- 1 onion, finely chopped
- 5 tbsp. oil
- 2 chopped garlic clove
- 2 chopped tomatoes
- Salt
- 1 tsp. sweet paprika
- A pinch of saffron
- 4 cleaned small squid, sliced
- 2 cups medium-grain brown rice
- 3 cups fish or chicken broth
- 1 cup dry white wine
- 12 jumbo shrimps
- 16 mussels, scrubbed and debearded

*Instructions*

Put ingredients in the slow cooker. Cover, and cook on low for 7 to 9 hours.

## Chicken & Green Beans Stew

*Serves 8*

*Ingredients - Allergies: SF, GF, DF, EF, NF*

- 2 cups green beans cut into 2 inch pieces
- 1 cup brown rice
- 1 cup chopped onions
- 2 tbsp. oil
- Salt, ground black pepper to taste
- 1 cup chicken stock
- 1 cup chopped tomato
- 1 Tbsp. parsley
- 4 pounds chicken breast meat cut into stripes

*Instructions*

Put ingredients in the slow cooker. Cover, and cook on low for 7 to 9 hours.

## Beef Liver Stew

*Serves 8*

*Ingredients - Allergies: SF, GF, DF, EF, NF*

- 2 cups chopped onions
- 2 tbsp. oil
- 3 garlic cloves, minced
- 3 grated carrots
- Salt, ground black pepper and ground cumin taste
- 2 cups chicken stock
- 1 cup red wine
- 1 tsp. turmeric (optional)
- 4 pounds Beef liver cut in stripes

*Instructions*

Put ingredients in the slow cooker. Cover, and cook on low for 7 to 9 hours.

## Beef, Leeks & Mushrooms Stew
*Serves 8*

*Ingredients - Allergies: SF, GF, DF, EF, NF*

- 2 cups chopped carrots
- 1 cup chopped onions
- 2 tbsp. oil
- 1 cup chopped leeks
- Salt & ground black pepper to taste
- 1 cup sliced mushrooms
- 1 cup sliced tomatoes
- 4 pounds beef meat cut into stripes

*Instructions*

Put ingredients in the slow cooker. Cover, and cook on low for 7 to 9 hours.

## Chicken & Butternut Squash Stew

*Serves 8*

*Ingredients - Allergies: SF, GF, DF, EF, NF*

- 3 cups cubed uncooked butternut squash
- 1 cup chopped onions
- 2 tbsp. oil
- 1 cup chopped red peppers
- Salt, ground black pepper to taste
- 1 cup chicken stock
- 4 pounds chicken dark, cubed

*Instructions*

Put ingredients in the slow cooker. Cover, and cook on low for 7 to 9 hours.

## Chicken & Brown Rice Stew

*Serves 8*

*Ingredients - Allergies: SF, GF, DF, EF, NF*

- 2 cups brown rice
- 2 cups chopped onions
- 2 tbsp. oil
- 1 cup chopped carrot
- Salt, ground black pepper and ground cumin to taste
- 4 cups chicken stock
- 4 pounds chicken pieces with skin on.
- ½ cup chopped caprsley and 8 kalamata olives

*Instructions*

Put ingredients in the slow cooker. Cover, and cook on low for 7 to 9 hours.

## Chicken, Garlic & Tomato Stew

*Serves 8*

*Ingredients - Allergies: SF, GF, DF, EF, NF*

- 3 cups tomatoes
- 2 cups chopped onions
- 2 tbsp. oil
- 1 garlic bulb, cut across
- Salt, ground black pepper and ground cumin to taste
- 1 Tbsp. minced garlic
- 4 pounds chicken breast meat cut into stripes

*Instructions*

Put ingredients in the slow cooker. Cover, and cook on low for 7 to 9 hours.

## Minced Pork, Tomato & Red Peppers Stew
*Serves 8*

*Ingredients - Allergies: SF, GF, DF, EF, NF*

- 3 cups quartered tomatoes
- 1 cup chopped onions
- 2 tbsp. oil
- 2 cups chopped red peppers
- Salt, ground black pepper and ground cumin to taste
- 1 cup shredded carrots
- 4 pounds minced pork meat

*Instructions*

Put ingredients in the slow cooker. Cover, and cook on low for 7 to 9 hours.

## Beef, Eggplant, Celery & Peppers Stew

*Serves 8*

*Ingredients - Allergies: SF, GF, DF, EF, NF*

- 1 cup cubed eggplant
- 2 cups chopped onions
- 2 tbsp. oil
- 1 cup sliced celery
- Salt, ground black pepper to taste
- 1 cup sliced red peppers
- 4 pounds beef meat cut into stripes

*Instructions*

Put ingredients in the slow cooker. Cover, and cook on low for 7 to 9 hours.

## Chicken & Onion Stew

*Serves 8*

*Ingredients - Allergies: SF, GF, DF, EF, NF*

- 1 cup sliced mushrooms
- 6 large onions, quartered
- 2 tbsp. oil
- Salt, ground black pepper to taste
- 2 cups chicken stock
- 4 pounds chicken drumsticks with skin on

*Instructions*

Put ingredients in the slow cooker. Cover, and cook on low for 7 to 9 hours.

## Pork & Black Eyed Peas Stew

*Serves 8*

*Ingredients - Allergies: SF, GF, DF, EF, NF*

- 1 cup chopped parsnips
- 2 cups chopped onions
- 2 tbsp. oil
- 1 cup uncooked black eyed peas
- 1 cup chopped tomato
- 1 cup chopped celery
- Salt, ground black pepper and ground cumin to taste
- 2 cups beef stock
- 4 pounds cubed pork meat

*Instructions*

Put ingredients in the slow cooker. Cover, and cook on low for 7 to 9 hours.

## Zucchini Rolls

*Serves 8*

*Ingredients - Allergies: SF, GF, DF, EF, NF*

- 1 cup brown rice
- 2 cups chopped onions
- 2 tbsp. oil
- 3-4 large zucchinis cut into thick stripes (see picture)
- Salt, ground black pepper and ground cumin to taste
- 2 cups beef stock
- 4 pounds minced beef meat

*Instructions*

Mix spices, meat, rice and onion, fill zucchini stripes with the mixture, make rolls and arrange them in the slow cooker. Add beef stock slowly by pouring by the sides. Cover, and cook on low for 7 to 9 hours.

# Beef Pot Roast with Broccoli

*Serves 8*

*Ingredients - Allergies: SF, GF, DF, EF, NF*

- 2 cups chopped onions
- 2 tbsp. coconut oil
- 3 cups broccoli
- Salt, ground black pepper & 2 bay leaves
- 2 cups beef stock
- 2 tsp. minced garlic
- 4 pounds beef pot roast

*Instructions*

Put ingredients in the slow cooker. Cover, and cook on low for 7 to 9 hours.

## Chicken and Sweet Potato

*Serves 8*

*Ingredients - Allergies: SF, GF, DF, EF, NF*

- 2 cups cubed sweet potato
- 2 cups chopped onions
- 2 tbsp. coconut oil
- 3 red peppers, chopped
- Salt, ground black pepper and ground cumin to taste
- 2 cups chicken stock
- 4 pounds chicken meat

*Instructions*

Put ingredients in the slow cooker. Cover, and cook on low for 7 to 9 hours.

## Jerk Chicken
*Serves 8*

*Ingredients - Allergies: SF, GF, DF, EF, NF*

- 2 cup sliced green peppers
- 2 cups chopped onions
- 2 tbsp. coconut oil
- Salt, ground black pepper and ground allspice to taste
- 2 cups chicken stock
- 4 pounds cubed chicken meat
- 1 lime - juice & 1 or more Scotch bonnet peppers (to taste).
- 2 Tbsp. minced ginger & 2 Tbsp. minced garlic.
- 1 Tsp. cinnamon & a pinch of nutmeg.

*Instructions*

Put ingredients in the slow cooker. Cover, and cook on low for 8 hours.

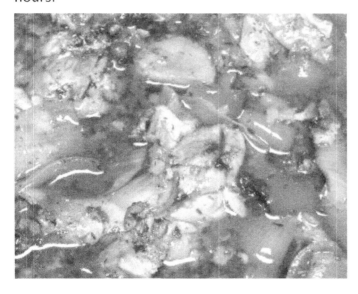

# Cauliflower Beef & Carrot

*Serves 8*

*Ingredients - Allergies: SF, GF, DF, EF, NF*

- 2 cup chopped carrots
- 2 cups chopped red onions
- 2 tbsp. coconut oil
- 2 cups cauliflower florets
- Salt, ground black pepper and ground cumin to taste
- 2 cups beef stock
- 4 pounds cubed beef meat

*Instructions*

Put ingredients in the slow cooker. Cover, and cook on low for 7 to 9 hours.

## Pork Broccoli

*Serves 8*

*Ingredients - Allergies: SF, GF, DF, EF, NF*

- 2 cups chopped onions
- 2 tbsp. coconut oil
- 3 cups broccoli
- Salt, ground black pepper and 1 Tbsp. chopped garlic
- 2 cups beef stock
- 4 pounds Pork roast

*Instructions*

Put ingredients in the slow cooker. Cover, and cook on low for 7 to 9 hours.

## Pork & Leeks

*Serves 8*

*Ingredients - Allergies: SF, GF, DF, EF, NF*

- 1 cup brown rice
- 2 cups chopped carrot
- 2 tbsp. <u>coconut</u> oil
- 3 cups chopped leeks
- Salt, ground black pepper and ground cumin to taste
- 2 cups beef stock
- 4 pounds cubed pork meat

*Instructions*

Put ingredients in the slow cooker. Cover, and cook on low for 7 to 9 hours.

## Mustard Chicken

*Serves 8*

*Ingredients - Allergies: SF, GF, DF, EF, NF*

- 1 cup chopped onions
- 1 cup chopped leeks
- 1 cup chopped mushrooms
- 2 tbsp. coconut oil
- Salt, ground black pepper
- 2 Tbsp. Mustard seeds (white and brown or black seeds)
- 1 cup chicken stock (3 cups if adding optional rice)
- 4 pounds cubed chicken meat
- 1 cup brown rice (optional). Rice will soak some liquid.

*Instructions*

Put ingredients in the slow cooker. Cover, and cook on low for 7 to 9 hours.

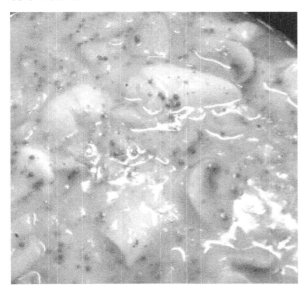

## Eggplant, Tripe & Broccoli

*Serves 8*

*Ingredients - Allergies: SF, GF, DF, EF, NF*

- 2 cups eggplant, sliced
- 1 cup chopped onions
- 1 cup broccoli
- 1 cup green beans
- 2 tbsp. coconut oil
- Salt, ground black pepper,
- 2 bay leaves & 2 Tbsp. chopped garlic
- 2 cups beef stock & 2 cups tomato paste
- 4 pounds beef tripe cut into stripes

*Instructions*

Put ingredients in the slow cooker. Cover, and cook on low for 9 hours.

## Cauliflower, Tomato and Minced Beef

*Serves 8*

*Ingredients - Allergies: SF, GF, DF, EF, NF*

- 2 cups chopped tomatoes
- 4 cups cauliflower florets
- 2 cups chopped onions
- 2 tbsp. coconut oil
- Salt, ground black pepper and cumin to taste
- 2 bay leaves & 2 Tbsp. chopped garlic & 1 tsp. oregano
- 2 cups beef stock & 1 cup tomato paste
- 4 pounds minced beef

*Instructions*

Put ingredients in the slow cooker. Cover, and cook on low for 9 hours.

## Kare Kare – oxtail stew

*Serves 8*

*Ingredients - Allergies: SF, GF, DF, EF, NF*

- 2 cups broccoli
- 1 cup green beans
- 2 cups chopped onions
- 2 tbsp. coconut oil
- Salt, ground black pepper and ground cumin to taste
- 2 bay leaves & 2 Tbsp. chopped garlic
- 2 cups beef stock & 2 cups tomato paste
- 4 pounds oxtail cut into 2 inch chunks

*Instructions*

Put ingredients in the slow cooker. Cover, and cook on low for 9 hours.

## Tuscan Pork & White Beans

*Serves 8*

*Ingredients - Allergies: SF, GF, DF, EF, NF*

- 1 cup tomatoes, sliced
- 2 cups chopped onions
- 2 cups kale or spinach
- 2 cups dry navy beans
- 2 tbsp. coconut oil
- Salt, ground black pepper and ground cumin to taste
- 2 bay leaves & 2 Tbsp. chopped garlic
- 2 cups beef stock
- 2 cups water
- 4 pounds pork shoulder meat

*Instructions*

Put ingredients in the slow cooker. Cover, and cook on low for 9 hours.

## Leeks, Mushrooms & Pork Neck Meat

*Serves 8*

*Ingredients - Allergies: SF, GF, DF, EF, NF*

• 2 cups mushrooms, sliced
• 2 cups chopped leeks
• 2 tbsp. coconut oil
• Salt, ground black pepper and ground cumin to taste
• 2 bay leaves & 2 Tbsp. chopped garlic
• 4 cups beef stock
• ¼ cup sesame seeds
• ¼ cup chopped spring onions
• 4 pounds pork neck meat

*Instructions*

Put all ingredients in the slow cooker except spring onions and sesame seeds. Cover, and cook on low for 9 hours. Sprinkle with chopped spring onions and sesame seeds.

## Beef, Beet, Carrots & Onions

*Serves 8*

*Ingredients - Allergies: SF, GF, DF, EF, NF*

- 2 cups julienned carrots
- 2 medium beets, peeled and sliced
- 2 cups chopped onions
- 2 tbsp. coconut oil
- Salt, ground black pepper to taste
- 2 cups beef stock
- 4 pounds cubed beef
- 2 Tbsp. minced garlic.

*Instructions*

Put ingredients in the slow cooker. Cover, and cook on low for 8 hours.

## Broccoli, Pork & Peppers
*Serves 8*

*Ingredients - Allergies: SF, GF, DF, EF, NF*

- 2 cup sliced yellow and orange peppers
- 1 cup chopped onions
- 2 tbsp. coconut oil
- Salt, ground black pepper to taste
- 1 cup beef stock
- 2 pounds pork chops
- 2 pounds pork neck
- 2 Tbsp. minced garlic.
- 2 cups broccoli florets

*Instructions*

Put ingredients in the slow cooker. Cover, and cook on low for 8 hours.

## Haitian Chicken Broccoli

*Serves 8*

*Ingredients - Allergies: SF, GF, DF, EF, NF*

- 2 cup broccoli florets
- 2 cups chopped onions
- 2 tbsp. coconut oil
- Salt, ground black pepper to taste
- 3 cups chicken stock
- 4 pounds cubed chicken meat
- 1 tsp. dried red pepper flakes (to taste).
- 4 whole cloves (discard after cooking)
- 2 Tbsp. minced garlic
- 1 Tbsp. apple vinegar

*Instructions*

Put ingredients in the slow cooker. Cover, and cook on low for 8 hours.

## Leeks, Cauliflower, Chicken & Carrot

*Serves 8*

*Ingredients - Allergies: SF, GF, DF, EF, NF*

- 3 cups sliced leeks
- 2 cups carrot
- 2 tbsp. coconut oil
- Salt, ground black pepper to taste
- 2 cups chicken stock
- 4 pounds cubed chicken meat
- 2 Tbsp. minced ginger & 2 Tbsp. minced garlic.
- 2 sticks celery, chopped

*Instructions*

Put ingredients in the slow cooker. Cover, and cook on low for 8 hours.

## Okra & Pork Stew
*Serves 8*

*Ingredients - Allergies: SF, GF, DF, EF, NF*

- 3 cups sliced okra
- 2 cups chopped onions
- 2 tbsp. coconut oil
- Salt, ground black pepper to taste
- 2 cups beef stock
- 4 pounds pork neck meat
- 5 cloves garlic, halved lengthwise
- 2 sticks celery, chopped

*Instructions*

Put ingredients in the slow cooker. Cover, and cook on low for 8 hours.

## Chicken, Black Beans and Cauliflower

*Serves 8*

*Ingredients - Allergies: SF, GF, DF, EF, NF*

- 2 cups cauliflower
- 1 cup black beans
- 2 cups chopped onions & 3 carrots - chopped
- 2 tbsp. coconut oil
- Salt, ground black pepper to taste
- 3 cups chicken stock
- 4 pounds dark chicken meat
- 2 Tbsp. minced garlic & 1 tsp. ground cumin

*Instructions*

Put ingredients in the slow cooker. Cover, and cook on low for 8 hours.

# Celery, Carrots & Cauliflower Pork
*Serves 8*

*Ingredients - Allergies: SF, GF, DF, EF, NF*

- 2 cup sliced celery
- 2 cups chopped onions
- 2 tbsp. coconut oil
- Salt, ground black pepper to taste
- 2 cups beef stock
- 4 pounds cubed pork meat
- 2 cups chopped carrots
- 2 cups chopped cauliflower
- 2 Tbsp. minced garlic & 3-4 bay leaves (discard after cooking).

*Instructions*

Put ingredients in the slow cooker. Cover, and cook on low for 8 hours.

## Slow Cooked Carnitas

*Serves 8*

*Ingredients - Allergies: SF, GF, DF, EF, NF*

- 2 cups chopped onions
- 2 tbsp. coconut oil
- Salt, ground black pepper to taste
- 2 pounds pork shoulder
- 2 pounds pork neck
- 1 Jalapeno pepper, chopped (to taste).
- 2 Tbsp. minced garlic.
- 1 Tbsp. ground cumin.

*Instructions*

Put ingredients in the slow cooker. Cover, and cook on low for 8 hours.

## Bigos- Polish Pork & Cabbage Stew
*Serves 8*

*Ingredients - Allergies: SF, GF, DF, EF, NF*

- 1 cup chopped onions
- 2 tbsp. coconut oil
- Salt, ground black pepper to taste
- 2 pound pork shoulder meat, cubed
- 2 pounds neck meat, cubed
- 3 cups shredded cabbage
- 2 Tbsp. minced garlic
- 1 Tbsp. ground paprika

*Instructions*

Put ingredients in the slow cooker. Cover, and cook on low for 8 hours.

## Cumin Pork

*Serves 8*

*Ingredients - Allergies: SF, GF, DF, EF, NF*

- 2 cups chopped onions
- 2 tbsp. coconut oil
- Salt, ground black pepper to taste
- 4 pounds pork meat, cubed
- 1 cup parsley
- 1 cup sesame seeds
- 2 Tbsp. minced garlic
- 3 Tbsp. ground cumin

*Instructions*

Put ingredients in the slow cooker. Cover, and cook on low for 8 hours.

## Mexican Pork Chili

*Serves 6*

*Ingredients - Allergies: SF, GF, DF, EF, NF*

- 2 tbsp. coconut oil
- 2 onions, chopped
- 3 cloves garlic, minced
- 3 pounds cubed pork meat
- 1 cup corn
- 1 cup tomato paste
- 2 cups beef broth
- 2 tbsp. cumin seeds
- 1 tsp. ground cayenne pepper
- 1 tsp. ground coriander
- 1 tsp. salt
- 3 cups cooked kidney beans
- 2-3 fresh hot chili peppers, chopped

*Instructions*

Put ingredients in the slow cooker. Cover, and cook on low for 8 hours.

# Superfoods Casseroles

Some recipes are for 1 person, adjust for 2 or more

## Chicken & Mushrooms Casserole

*Serves 2*

*Ingredients - Allergies: SF, GF, DF, EF, NF*

- 1 large onion, chopped
- 3 cups sliced mushrooms
- 2 tbsp. oil
- 1/2 tsp. salt
- 1/4 tsp. ground black pepper
- 1/2 tsp. minced garlic
- 2 large chicken breast pieces with skin on

*Instructions*

Oil casserole dish with oil, put chicken pieces in. Mix onion, salt, pepper, mushrooms and garlic and put over chicken. Cover and bake for 1 ½ hours on 400F.

## Pork & Red Peppers Casserole

*Serves 8*

*Ingredients - Allergies: SF, GF, NF*

- 1 cup chopped onions
- 2 cups sliced Red Peppers
- 4 pounds cubed pork
- 1 cup "healthy casserole sauce"

*Instructions*

Put all ingredients in the casserole dish, pour sauce on top, cover and bake for 2 hours on 400F. Garnish with parsley.

## Chicken, Carrot and Cherry Tomatoes Casserole

*Serves 8*

*Ingredients - Allergies: SF, GF, DF, EF, NF*

- 1-1/2 cups chopped carrots
- 1 cup chopped onions
- 2 tbsp. oil
- 1-1/2 cups yellow peppers
- 1/2 tsp. salt
- 1/4 tsp. ground black pepper
- 1/2 tsp. minced garlic
- 4 pounds cubed chicken
- 1/2 cups chopped parsley

*Instructions*

Put all ingredients in the casserole dish, cover and bake for 2 hours on 400F.

## Chicken, Carrot and Onions Italian Casserole

*Serves 6*

*Ingredients - Allergies: SF, GF, DF, EF, NF*

- 1-1/2 cups chopped carrots
- 1 cup chopped onions
- 2 tbsp. oil
- 1 cup sliced mushrooms
- 1/2 tsp. salt
- 1/4 tsp. ground black pepper
- 1/2 tsp. minced garlic
- 1 tsp. fresh rosemary
- 4 pounds chicken with skin on

*Instructions*

Put all ingredients in the casserole dish, cover and bake for 2 hours on 400F.

# Red Peppers, Zucchini and Eggplant Casserole

*Serves 8*

*Ingredients - Allergies: SF, GF, DF, EF, NF*

- 1 chopped carrots
- 1 - 1/2 cup chopped onions
- 1 - 1/2 cup sliced red peppers
- 2 tbsp. oil
- 1 cup sliced zucchini
- 1/2 tsp. salt
- 1/4 tsp. ground black pepper
- 1/2 tsp. minced garlic
- 1/2 tsp. oregano
- 2 pounds sliced eggplant

*Instructions*

Put all ingredients in the casserole dish, cover and bake for 2 hours on 400F.

## Chicken, Olives & Garlic Casserole
*Serves 8*

*Ingredients - Allergies: SF, GF, DF, EF, NF*

- 1 cup chopped onions
- 2 tbsp. oil
- 1 cup Kalamata olives
- 1/4 tsp. ground black pepper
- 1 head garlic, sliced across (bake separately for 45 minutes)
- 1 Tbsp. fresh rosemary
- 4 pounds chicken pieces (dark meat) with skin on

*Instructions*

Put chicken, onions and olives in the casserole dish, season, cover and bake for 2 hours on 400F. Serve with baked garlic.

## Shrimp, Tomato Paste and Red Peppers Casserole

*Serves 4*

*Ingredients - Allergies: SF, GF, DF, EF, NF*

- 1/2 cups chopped carrots
- 1 cup chopped red peppers
- 1/2 cup chopped onions
- 2 tbsp. oil
- 2 cups tomato paste - see recipe at the beginning
- 1/2 tsp. salt
- 1/4 tsp. ground black pepper
- 1 tsp. minced garlic
- 2 pounds shrimp

*Instructions*

Put all ingredients in the casserole dish, cover and bake for 2 hours on 400F.

## Pork Chop Casserole

*Serves 1*

*Ingredients - Allergies: SF, GF, DF, EF, NF*

- 3 cups vegetable broth
- 1 cup brown rice
- 5 ounce mushrooms
- salt and pepper to taste
- 6 (3/4 inch) thick pork chops

*Instructions*

Heat oven to 350F. Pour broth into a baking dish. Add rice and mushrooms and mix. Salt and pepper to taste. Add pork chops in a single layer on that mixture and push them down into mixture and make sure they are covered with it.
Cover baking dish with aluminum foil and bake for 1 hour.

Chicken Eggplant Casserole

*Ingredients – serves 4 - Allergies: SF, GF, NF*

- 3 pounds Eggplant
- Salt and ground black pepper
- 1 tbsp. chopped parsley
- 2 beaten eggs
- 1 cup of low-fat Greek yogurt
- 1/2 cup of shredded cheddar cheese, low-fat
- 1 pound cubed skinless boneless chicken (or turkey) breasts

*Instructions*

Preheat oven to 375 degrees F. Mix beaten eggs and low-fat yogurt in a separate dish. In a casserole, place 1 layer of eggplant and meat cubes. Sprinkle with salt, pepper, and parsley. Cover with 1/2 of a cup of eggs/yogurt mixture. Repeat process 2 more times and cover with shredded cheese. Bake until eggplant and chicken are tender and crust is golden brown, about 20 minutes. Serve with Large Fiber Loaded salad with Italian Dressing.

## Salmon Broccoli Casserole

*Serves 4*

*Ingredients - Allergies: SF, GF, NF*

- 2 cups broccoli florets
- 1/2 cup chopped onions
- 2 tbsp. oil
- 2 cups healthy casserole sauce
- 1/2 tsp. salt
- 1/4 tsp. ground black pepper
- 1 tsp. minced garlic
- 2 pounds slamon steaks, quartered

*Instructions*

Put all recipe ingredients but sauce in the casserole dish, pour sauce on top, cover and bake for 2 hours on 400F.

# Zucchini Noodles & Slivered Almonds Casserole

*Serves 4*

*Ingredients - Allergies: SF, GF, DF, EF, NF*

- 1/2 cups chopped carrots
- 5 cups raw zucchini noodles (use spiralizer)
- 1/2 cup chopped onions
- 2 cups toasted slivered almonds
- 2 tbsp. oil
- 1/2 tsp. salt
- 1/4 tsp. ground black pepper

*Instructions*

Put all recipe ingredients in the casserole dish, cover and bake for 45 minutes on 400F.

# Lamb & Spinach Casserole

*Serves 4*

*Ingredients - Allergies: SF, GF, NF*

- 1/2 cups chopped carrots
- 3 cups spinach
- 1 cup chopped onions
- 1/2 cup sliced leeks
- 2 tbsp. oil
- 2 cups healthy casserole sauce
- 1/2 tsp. salt
- 1/4 tsp. ground black pepper
- 2 tsp. minced garlic
- 2 pounds cubed lamb meat
- 1 tbsp. minced parsley for garnishing

*Instructions*

Put all recipe ingredients in the casserole dish but sauce, pour sauce over, cover and bake for 2 hours on 400F.

# Chicken, Zucchini and Cherry Tomatoes Casserole

*Serves 4*

*Ingredients - Allergies: SF, GF, NF*

- 2 cups cherry tomatoes
- 1/2 cup chopped leeks
- 2 tbsp. oil
- 2 cups sliced zucchini
- 1 cup healthy casserole sauce
- 1/2 tsp. salt
- 1/4 tsp. ground black pepper
- 2 tsp. minced garlic
- 2 pounds chicken

*Instructions*

Put all recipe ingredients but sauce in the casserole dish, pour sauce over, cover and bake for 2 hours on 400F.

## Spinach Casserole

*Serves 4*

*Ingredients - Allergies: SF, GF, EF, NF*

- 5 cups spinach
- 8 eggs, whipped
- 1/2 cup chopped onions
- 2 tbsp. oil
- 2 cups thick plain Greek Yogurt
- 1/2 tsp. salt
- 1/4 tsp. ground black pepper
- 2 tsp. minced garlic

*Instructions*

Mix all ingredients but yogurt together, put in the casserole dish, cover and bake for 1 hour on 400F. Add yogurt and mix before serving.

# Bonus Chapter – Superfoods Condiments

## Basil Pesto

- 1 cup basil
- 1/3 cup cashews
- 2 garlic cloves, chopped
- 1/2 cup olive oil

Process basil, cashews and garlic until smooth. Add oil in a slow stream. Process to combine. Transfer to a bowl. Season with salt and pepper. Stir to combine.  Allergies: SF, GF, DF, EF, V

## Cilantro Pesto

- 1 cup cilantro
- 1/3 cup cashews
- 2 garlic cloves, chopped
- 1/2 cup olive oil

Process cilantro, cashews and garlic. Add oil in a slow stream. Process to combine. Transfer to a bowl. Season with salt and pepper. Stir to combine. Allergies: SF, GF, DF, EF, V

## Sundried Tomato Pesto

- 3/4 cup sundried tomatoes
- 1/3 cup cashews
- 2 garlic cloves, chopped
- 1/2 cup olive oil

Process tomato, cashews and garlic. Add oil in a slow stream. Process to combine. Transfer to a bowl. Season with salt and pepper. Stir to combine. Allergies: SF, GF, DF, EF, V

## Sweets

### Vegan Superfoods Stuffed Apples

*Filling Ingredients*

- 1 cup ground cashews
- 1 tsp. of ground vanilla bean
- 1/2 cup oil
- 1/4 cup honey
- 2 tbsp. flax meal
- 2 tbsp. cacao powder

*Instructions*

Mix all filling ingredients. Core 10 apples, fill them with filling mix, put them in the slow cooker and cook on low for 2 hours.

## Vegan Superfoods Granola

*Ingredients*

- 10 Cup Rolled Oats
- 1/2 Pound Shredded Coconut
- 2 Cup Raw Sunflower Seeds
- 1 Cup Sesame Seeds
- 3 Cup Chopped Nuts
- 1-1/2 Cup -Water
- 1-1/2 Cup oil
- 1 Cup honey
- 1-1/2 Tsp. Salt
- 2 Tsp. Cinnamon
- 1 tbsp. of ground vanilla bean
- Dried cranberries

*Instructions*

Combine oats, coconut, sunflower seeds, sesame seed, cranberries and nuts (can include almonds, pecans, walnuts, or a combination of all of them). Blend well and put them in slow cooker dish.

Combine water, oil, raw honey, salt, cinnamon and vanilla in a large pan. Heat until raw honey is dissolved, but don't boil.

Pour the honey over the dry ingredients and stir well. Cook on low for 2 Hours.

## Banana Carrot Bread

*Ingredients*

- 2 cups flour
- 1/3 cup honey
- 2 teaspoons cinnamon
- 2 teaspoons baking powder
- 1/2 teaspoon baking soda
- Pinch of sea salt
- 1/2 cup milk at the room temperature
- 1/4 cup warmed oil
- 3 mashed bananas
- 3 carrots, grated
- 3/4 cup chopped walnuts

*Instructions*

Preheat oven to 350 degrees F. In a large mixing bowl, add flour, honey, cinnamon, baking powder, soda and salt and mix well. Add almond milk, oil, hemp hearts, mashed bananas and mix. Add carrots. Put the mixture in the slow cooker and cook on high for 2 hours or 4 hours on low.

Let cool for 10 minutes, remove from pan and let cool completely. Store covered. Serve warmed or at room temperature. Slices would pair nicely with this Cashew Sweet Cream.

# Upside down Apple Cake

### Ingredients

Bottom Fruit Layer:

- 2 tbsp. oil melted
- 1 apple, sliced, or 1/4 cup blueberries, plums, banana etc.
- 2 tbsp. walnut chunks
- 2 tbsp. sugar
- 1 tsp ground cinnamon.

Top Cake Layer:

- 1/3 cup honey
- 1/4 cup milk.
- 1 tsp ground vanilla bean
- 1 tsp lemon juice.
- 1 banana, mashed, or 1/4 cup blueberries
- 1/3 cup flour

### Instructions

Place 2 tbsps. oil into slow cooker pan. Sprinkle 2 tbsps. sugar all over the oil. Sprinkle 1 tsp cinnamon on top of sweetened layer.

Layer apple slices or blueberries on top of sweetened layer. Add walnut pieces to fruit layer. Set aside.

Combine all the "top cake layer" ingredients in a large mixing bowl except for the coconut flour. Mix and add the flour and mix well.

Spoon batter on top of fruit layer and spread evenly.

Cook on low for 4 hours.

## Cheese, Eggs & Raspberry Casserole
*Serves 4-6*

*Ingredients - Allergies: SF, GF, NF*

- 1 cup low fat farmers cheese
- 1 cup low fat cream cheese
- 1 cup honey
- 1 cup low fat sour cream
- 2 large eggs + 3 egg whites
- 2 tablespoons flour
- 1 tsp. ground vanilla bean
- 1 cup raspberries
- 1/2 cup black currants or blueberries

*Instructions*

Preheat the oven to 350 F. Beat both cheeses, honey and sour cream until smooth (few minutes). Whisk egg whites in a bowl and then add to the cheese mixture along with 2 whole eggs, almond flour, ground vanilla bean and lemon zest. Beat on medium speed for 3 minutes and pour in the oiled casserole dish.

Put strawberries and black currants on top and bake until the cake is set (approx. 60-70 minutes). Turn off the oven and keep the cheesecake inside for 15 minutes.

## Oatmeal, Walnuts and Cranberry Casserole

*Serves 6*

*Ingredients - Allergies: SF, GF, DF, EF, NF*

- 2 cups oats
- 1/2 cup honey
- 1 tsp. cinnamon
- 1 tsp. baking powder
- 1/2 tsp. salt
- 1 cup walnuts
- 1 egg
- 1/2 cup blueberries
- 1/2 cup raspberries
- 2 cups milk
- 3 Tbsp. oil
- 1 Tbsp. ground vanilla bean

*Instructions*

Preheat oven to 375 and oil the casserole dish.

Mix oats, honey, cinnamon, baking powder, salt, walnuts and berries. Whisk together the milk, egg, oil and vanilla in another bowl. Put the oat mixture to the casserole dish and pour milk mixture.

Bake approx. 40 minutes.

## Oats & Blueberry Cake

### Ingredients

- 2 1/2 cups old-fashioned rolled oats
- 1 1/2 cups milk
- 1/3 cup honey
- 2 tablespoons oil
- 1 teaspoon ground vanilla bean
- 1 teaspoon ground cinnamon
- 1 teaspoon baking powder
- 1/4 teaspoon salt
- 3/4 cup blueberries

Instructions

Combine oats and almond milk, cover and let soak in the fridge overnight.

Stir egg, honey, oil, vanilla, cinnamon, salt and baking powder into the oats until well combined. Mix in blueberries. Pour into oiled slow cooker dish.

Cook on low for 4 hous. Top with blueberries and raspberries and serve warm.

# Superfoods Reference Book

Unfortunately, I had to take out the whole Superfoods Reference Book out of all of my books because parts of that book are featured on my blog. I joined Kindle Direct Publishing Select program which allows me to have all my books free for 5 days every 3 months. Unfortunately, KDP Select program also means that all my books have to have unique content that is not available in any other online store or on the Internet (including my blog). I didn't want to remove parts of Superfoods Reference book that is already on my blog because I want that all people have free access to that information. I also wanted to be part of KDP Select program because that is an option to give my book for free to anyone. So, some sections of my Superfoods Reference Book can be found on my blog, under Superfoods menu on my blog. Complete Reference book is available for subscribers to my Superfoods Today Newsletter. Subscribers to my Newsletter will also get information whenever any of my books becomes free on Amazon. I will not offer any product pitches or anything similar to my subscribers, only Superfoods related information, recipes and weight loss and fitness tips. So, subscribe to my newsletter, download Superfoods Today Desserts free eBook which has complete Superfood Reference book included and have the opportunity to get all of my future books for free.

## Your Free Gift

As a way of saying thanks for your purchase, I'm offering you my FREE eBook that is exclusive to my book and blog readers.

Superfoods Cookbook Book Two has over 70 Superfoods recipes and complements Superfoods Cookbook Book One and it contains Superfoods Salads, Superfoods Smoothies and Superfoods Deserts with ultra-healthy non-refined ingredients. All ingredients are 100% Superfoods.

It also contains Superfoods Reference book which is organized by Superfoods (more than 60 of them, with the list of their benefits), Superfoods spices, all vitamins, minerals and antioxidants. Superfoods Reference Book lists Superfoods that can help with 12 diseases and 9 types of cancer.

http://www.SuperfoodsToday.com/FREE

# Other Books from this Author

*Superfoods Today Diet* is a Kindle Superfoods Diet [book](book) that gives you 4 week Superfoods Diet meal plan as well as 2 weeks maintenance meal plan and recipes for weight loss success. It is an extension of Detox book and it's written for people who want to switch to Superfoods lifestyle.

*Superfoods Today Body Care* is a Kindle [book](book) with over 50 Natural Recipes for beautiful skin and hair. It has body scrubs, facial masks and hair care recipes made with the best Superfoods like avocado honey, coconut, olive oil, oatmeal, yogurt, banana and Superfoods herbs like lavender, rosemary, mint, sage, hibiscus, rose.

*Superfoods Today Cookbook* is a Kindle book that contains over 160 Superfoods recipes created with 100% Superfoods ingredients. Most of the meals can be prepared in under 30 minutes and some are really quick ones that can be done in 10 minutes only. Each recipe combines Superfoods ingredients that deliver astonishing amounts of antioxidants, essential fatty acids (like omega-3), minerals, vitamins, and more.

*Superfoods Today Smoothies* is a Kindle Superfoods Smoothies book with over 70+ 100% Superfoods smoothies. Featured are Red, Purple, Green and Yellow Smoothies

*Superfoods Today Salads* is a Kindle book that contains over 60 Superfoods Salads recipes created with 100% Superfoods ingredients. Most of the salads can be prepared in 10 minutes and most are measured for two. Each recipe combines Superfoods ingredients that deliver astonishing amounts of antioxidants, essential fatty acids (like omega-3), minerals, vitamins, and more.

*Superfoods Today Kettlebells* is a Kindle Kettlebells beginner's book aimed at 30+ office workers who want to improve their health and build stronger body without fat.

**Superfoods Today Red Smoothies** is a Kindle Superfoods Smoothies book with more than 40 Red Smoothies.

**Superfoods Today 14 Days Detox** is a Kindle Superfoods Detox book that gives you 2 week Superfoods Detox meal plan and recipes for Detox success.

**Superfoods Today Yellow Smoothies** is a Kindle Superfoods Smoothies book with more than 40 Yellow Smoothies.

**Superfoods Today Green Smoothies** is a Kindle Superfoods Smoothies book with more than 35 Green Smoothies.

*Superfoods Today Purple Smoothies* is a Kindle Superfoods Smoothies book with more than 40 Purple Smoothies.

*Superfoods Cooking For Two* is a Kindle book that contains over 150 Superfoods recipes for two created with 100% Superfoods ingredients.

**Nighttime Eater** is a Kindle book that deals with Nighttime Eating Syndrome (NES). Don Orwell is a life-long Nighttime Eater that has lost his weight with Superfoods and engineered a solution around Nighttime Eating problem. Don still eats at night☺. Don't fight your nature, you can continue to eat at night, be binge free and maintain low weight.

**Superfoods Today Smart Carbs 20 Days Detox** is a Kindle Superfoods book that will teach you how to detox your body and start losing weight with Smart Carbs. The book has over 470+ pages with over 160+ 100% Superfoods recipes.

*Superfoods Today Vegetarian Salads* is a Kindle book that contains over 40 Superfoods Vegetarian Salads recipes created with 100% Superfoods ingredients. Most of the salads can be prepared in 10 minutes and most are measured for two.

*Superfoods Today Vegan Salads* is a Kindle book that contains over 30 Superfoods Vegan Salads recipes created with 100% Superfoods ingredients. Most of the salads can be prepared in 10 minutes and most are measured for two.

**Superfoods Today Soups & Stews** is a Kindle book that contains over 70 Superfoods Soups and Stews recipes created with 100% Superfoods ingredients.

**Superfoods Desserts** is a Kindle Superfoods Desserts book with more than 60 Superfoods Recipes.

**Smoothies for Diabetics** is a Kindle book that contains over 70 Superfoods Smoothies adjusted for diabetics.

**50 Shades of Superfoods for Two** is a Kindle book that contains over 150 Superfoods recipes for two created with 100% Superfoods ingredients.

*50 Shades of Smoothies* is a Kindle book that contains over 70 Superfoods Smoothies.

*50 Shades of Superfoods Salads* is a Kindle book that contains over 60 Superfoods Salads recipes created with 100% Superfoods ingredients. Most of the salads can be prepared in 10 minutes and most are measured for two. Each recipe combines Superfoods ingredients that deliver astonishing amounts of antioxidants, essential fatty acids (like omega-3), minerals, vitamins, and more.

**Superfoods Vegan Desserts** is a Kindle Vegan Dessert <u>book</u> with 100% Vegan Superfoods Recipes.

**Desserts for Two** is a Kindle Superfoods Desserts <u>book</u> with more than 40 Superfoods Desserts Recipes for two.

**Superfoods Paleo Cookbook** is a Kindle Paleo <u>book</u> with more than 150 100% Superfoods Paleo Recipes.

**Superfoods Breakfasts** is a Kindle Superfoods <u>book</u> with more than 40 100% Superfoods Breakfasts Recipes.

**Superfoods Dump Dinners** is a Kindle Superfoods <u>book</u> with Superfoods Dump Dinners Recipes.

**Healthy Desserts** is a Kindle Desserts <u>book</u> with more than 50 100% Superfoods Healthy Desserts Recipes.

**Superfoods Salads in a Jar** is a Kindle Salads in a Jar book with more than 35 100% Superfoods Salads Recipes.

**Smoothies for Kids** is a Kindle Smoothies book with more than 80 100% Superfoods Smoothies for Kids Recipes.

***Vegan Cookbook for Beginners*** is a Kindle Vegan <u>book</u> with more than 75 100% Superfoods Vegan Recipes.

***Vegetarian Cooking for Beginners*** is a Kindle Vegetarian <u>book</u> with more than 150 100% Superfoods Paleo Recipes.

**_Foods for Diabetics_** is a Kindle <u>book</u> with more than 170 100% Superfoods Diabetics Recipes.

Made in the USA
Las Vegas, NV
04 December 2023

82054031R00142